FRANCIS FRITH'S

UTTOXETER

LIVING MEMORIES

The compilation of text in this book is a team effort combining the knowledge and experience of **UTTOXETER CIVIC SOCIETY**. The Civic Society was re-established in 2004 after an absence of over 20 years in the town. As Uttoxeter is currently going through a process of regeneration through the Market Towns initiative, it was thought prudent that this civic 'watch dog' organisation was re-introduced to scrutinise and moderate developments in the town. A number of individual members of the Civic Society have contributed to the development of the text in this volume. A very special thanks to Tom Parkes for his central role in this project and in providing us with access to his unparalleled local knowledge of history and heritage.

**FRANCIS FRITH'S
PHOTOGRAPHIC MEMORIES**

UTTOXETER
LIVING MEMORIES

UTTOXETER CIVIC SOCIETY

First published in the United Kingdom in 2005 by The Francis
Frith Collection®

Hardback edition published in 2005 ISBN 1-84589-018-3

Paperback edition 2005 ISBN 1-85937-963-X

British Library Cataloguing in Publication Data

Uttoxeter - Living Memories
Uttoxeter Civic Society

The Francis Frith Collection
Frith's Barn, Teffont,
Salisbury, Wiltshire SP3 5QP
Tel: +44 (0) 1722 716 376
Email: info@francisfrith.co.uk
www.francisfrith.co.uk

Printed and bound in Great Britain

Front Cover: UTTOXETER, *Market Place c1955* U29015t
Frontispiece: UTTOXETER, *Market Place c1965* U29059

*The colour-tinting is for illustrative purposes only, and is not intended to be
historically accurate*

Aerial photographs reproduced under licence from
Simmons Aerofilms Limited.
Historical Ordnance Survey maps reproduced under licence from
Homecheck.co.uk

Every attempt has been made to contact copyright holders of
illustrative material. We will be happy to give full acknowledgement in
future editions for any items not credited. Any information should be
directed to The Francis Frith Collection.

AS WITH ANY HISTORICAL DATABASE THE FRITH ARCHIVE IS
CONSTANTLY BEING CORRECTED AND IMPROVED AND THE
PUBLISHERS WOULD WELCOME INFORMATION ON OMISSIONS OR INACCURACIES

CONTENTS

FRANCIS FRITH: VICTORIAN PIONEER   7

UTTOXETER - AN INTRODUCTION   10

UTTOXETER FROM THE AIR   16

UTTOXETER LIVING MEMORIES   18

STAFFORDSHIRE COUNTY MAP   70

INDEX   89

NAMES OF PRE-PUBLICATION BUYERS   90

Free Mounted Print Voucher   93

FRANCIS FRITH
VICTORIAN PIONEER

FRANCIS FRITH, founder of the world-famous pho-tographic archive, was a complex and multi-tal-ented man. A devout Quaker and a highly successful Victorian businessman, he was philosophical by nature and pioneering in outlook.

By 1855 he had already established a wholesale grocery business in Liverpool, and sold it for the astonishing sum of £200,000, which is the equiva-lent today of over £15,000,000. Now a very rich man, he was able to indulge his passion for travel. As a child he had pored over travel books written by early explorers, and his fancy and imagination had been stirred by family holidays to the sublime mountain regions of Wales and Scotland. 'What lands of spirit-stirring and enriching scenes and places!' he had written. He was to return to these scenes of grandeur in later years to 'recapture the thousands of vivid and tender memories', but with a different purpose. Now in his thirties, and captivated by the new sci-ence of photography, Frith set out on a series of pioneering journeys up the Nile and to the Near East that occupied him from 1856 unti 1860.

INTRIGUE AND EXPLORATION

These far-flung journeys were packed with intrigue and adventure. In his life story, written when he was sixty-three, Frith tells of being held captive by bandits, and of fighting 'an awful midnight battle to the very point of surrender with a deadly pack of hungry, wild dogs'. Wearing flowing Arab costume, Frith arrived at Akaba by camel sixty years before Lawrence of Arabia, where he encountered 'desert princes and rival sheikhs, blazing with jewel-hilted swords'.

He was the first photographer to venture beyond the sixth cataract of the Nile. Africa was still the mysterious 'Dark Continent', and Stanley and Livingstone's historic meeting was a decade into the future. The conditions for picture taking confound belief. He laboured for hours in his wicker dark-room in the sweltering heat of the desert, while the volatile chemicals fizzed dangerously in their trays. Back in London he exhibited his photographs and was 'rapturously cheered' by members of the Royal Society. His reputation as a photographer was made overnight.

VENTURE OF A LIFE-TIME

Characteristically, Frith quickly spotted the opportu-nity to create a new business as a specialist publish-er of photographs. He lived in an era of immense and sometimes violent change. For the poor in the early part of Victoria's reign work was exhausting and the hours long, and people had precious little free time to enjoy themselves. Most people had no transport other than a cart or gig at their disposal, and rarely

travelled far beyond the boundaries of their own town or village. However, by the 1870s the railways had threaded their way across the country, and Bank Holidays and half-day Saturdays had been made obligatory by Act of Parliament. All of a sudden the working man and his family were able to enjoy days out and see a little more of the world.

With typical business acumen, Francis Frith foresaw that these new tourists would enjoy having souvenirs to commemorate their days out. In 1860 he married Mary Ann Rosling and set out on a new career: his aim was to photograph every city, town and village in Britain. For the next thirty years he travelled the country by train and by pony and trap, producing fine photographs of seaside resorts and beauty spots that were keenly bought by millions of Victorians. These prints were painstakingly pasted into family albums and pored over during the dark nights of winter, rekindling precious memories of summer excursions.

THE RISE OF FRITH & CO

Frith's studio was soon supplying retail shops all over the country. To meet the demand he gathered about him a small team of photographers, and published the work of independent artist-photographers of the calibre of Roger Fenton and Francis Bedford. In order to gain some understanding of the scale of

Frith's business one only has to look at the catalogue issued by Frith & Co in 1886: it runs to some 670 pages, listing not only many thousands of views of the British Isles but also many photographs of most European countries, and China, Japan, the USA and Canada - note the sample page shown on page 9 from the hand-written Frith & Co ledgers recording the pictures. By 1890 Frith had created the greatest specialist photographic publishing company in the world, with over 2,000 sales outlets - more than the combined number that Boots and WH Smith have today! The picture on the next page shows the Frith & Co display board at Ingleton in the Yorkshire Dales (left of window). Beautifully constructed with a mahogany frame and gilt inserts, it could display up to a dozen local scenes.

POSTCARD BONANZA

The ever-popular holiday postcard we know today took many years to develop. In 1870 the Post Office issued the first plain cards, with a pre-printed stamp on one face. In 1894 they allowed other publishers' cards to be sent through the mail with an attached adhesive halfpenny stamp. Demand grew rapidly, and in 1895 a new size of postcard was permitted called the court card, but there was little room for illustration. In 1899, a year after Frith's death, a new card measuring 5.5 x 3.5 inches became the standard format, but it was not until 1902 that the divided back came into being, so that the address and message could be on one face and a full-size illustration on the other. Frith & Co were in the vanguard of postcard development: Frith's sons Eustace and Cyril continued their father's monumental task, expanding the number of views offered to the public and recording more and more places in Britain, as the coasts and countryside were opened up to mass travel.

Francis Frith had died in 1898 at his villa in Cannes, his great project still growing. The archive he created continued in business for another seventy years. By 1970 it contained over a third of a million pictures showing 7,000 British towns and villages.

5	.	*illegible College, view from the garden*			+
6	.	St Catherine's College		+	
7	.	Senate House & Library		+	
8	.			+	
3 0	.	Garrard Hostel Bridge		+	+ +
	.	Geological Museum		+	
1	.	Addenbrookes Hospital		+	
2	.	St Mary's Church		+	
3	.	Fitzwilliam Museum, Pitt Press &c		+	
4	.			+	
5	Buxton, The Crescent				+
6	.	The Colonnade			+
7	.	Public Gardens			+
8	.				+
3 9	.				+
4 0	Haddon Hall, View from the Terrace				+
	Millers Dale				+
1	Bakewell, Bridge &c				+
2	.	Footbridge			+
3	.	Church			+
4	.	" Interior			+
5	Matlock Bath, The High Tor				+
6	.	On the Derwent			+
7	.	" Brunswood Terrace			+
8	.	Cliffs &c			+

FRANCIS FRITH'S LEGACY

Frith's legacy to us today is of immense significance and value, for the magnificent archive of evocative photographs he created provides a unique record of change in the cities, towns and villages throughout Britain over a century and more. Frith and his fellow studio photographers revisited locations many times down the years to update their views, compiling for us an enthralling and colourful pageant of British life and character.

We are fortunate that Frith was dedicated to recording the minutiae of everyday life, for it is this sheer wealth of visual data, the painstaking chronicle of changes in dress, transport, street layouts, buildings, housing, engineering and landscape that captivates us so much today. His remarkable images offer us a powerful link with the past and with the lives of our ancestors.

THE VALUE OF THE ARCHIVE TODAY

Computers have now made it possible for Frith's many thousands of images to be accessed almost instantly. Frith's images are increasingly used as visual resources, by social historians, by researchers into genealogy and ancestry, by architects and town planners, and by teachers involved in local history projects.

In addition, the archive offers every one of us an opportunity to examine the places where we and our families have lived and worked down the years. Highly successful in Frith's own era, the archive is now, a century and more on, entering a new phase of popularity. Historians consider the Francis Frith Collection to be of prime national importance. It is the only archive of its kind remaining in private ownership. Francis Frith's archive is now housed in an historic timber barn in the beautiful village of Teffont in Wiltshire. Its founder would not recognize the archive office as it is today. In place of the many thousands of dusty boxes containing glass plate negatives and an all-pervading odour of photographic chemicals, there are now ranks of computer screens. He would be amazed to watch his images travelling round the world at unimaginable speeds through internet lines.

The archive's future is both bright and exciting. Francis Frith, with his unshakeable belief in making photographs available to the greatest number of people, would undoubtedly approve of what is being done today with his lifetime's work. His photographs depicting our shared past are now bringing pleasure and enlightenment to millions around the world a century and more after his death.

UTTOXETER
AN INTRODUCTION

UTTOXETER is a typical English market town. Situated on a bluff above the valley of the River Dove on the borders of Staffordshire and Derbyshire, it has always occupied a strategic position for all routes through the ages. Today it occupies a convenient central situation on the busy A50, which links the M1 and M6. It is ideally situated, for it is close to many large Midlands towns and cities, and Manchester and Sheffield are within easy reach. Its population has increased significantly in the past few years, and is now around thirteen thousand.

ORIGINS

The whole heavily wooded areas of the Dove Valley slopes and the steep-sided Picknall or Hockley Valley to the south would have provided much to attract prehistoric seasonal travellers. Indeed, there are recorded finds of stone tools and artefacts in this area, whilst up on the raised area of the Heath, near the old Elkes Sports Ground, a fine example of a Bronze Age palstave axe was found. This axe is now proudly displayed in

HIGH STREET *c1955* U29004

Hanley museum; it was the subject of a tug of war between Uttoxeter and Hanley for some years, with Uttoxeter claiming that the axe's rightful place was in Uttoxeter Heritage Centre.

There is sufficient evidence to suggest that the town's central area - historically called Bare or Bear Hill on Thomas Lightfoot's 1658 map - was probably a good defensive position in relation to the River Dove in the period before AD 600, and some commentators also allude to a British hill settlement here. It has been suggested that the Romans probably made use of this settlement as a fort to command the important river route of the Dove at that time in history, or at least to control a strategic river crossing. This defensive position would have been in plain view of the forts at Rocester and Tutbury, and it was ideally placed at an elevated position in the bend of the wide river valley.

Recent evidence has come to light of at least a Roman villa in the area, and also a Roman road. This road's destination is as yet uncertain; it runs south from the Rocester area to Stramshall and possibly to the Parks area of Uttoxeter, where a Roman hoard was discovered in the 1970s. The highly fertile river valley could well have supported a very large agricultural and industrial settlement (this is what Roman villas were), and it could also have fed the successive Roman military forts which existed at Rocester from around AD 70 to AD 400.

Uttoxeter ancient history is hazy, but it now seems likely that it has evolved from two settlement centres established at different times: Bare Hill on the edge of the Dove Valley, and the uplands of the Heath. These eventually became joined along the High Street, or 'Old Road' as it was previously called, which runs due north and joins the two. Although the Uttoxeter area was sparsely populated in the Iron Age, Celts must have settled here, for the confluence of three major tribal territories was nearby. Uttoxeter's historian Francis Redfern recalls the excavation of an Ogham stone from the ancient Maidens' Well in 1870. Ogham carvings are a rudimentary linear script, and this stone could possibly have been used as a tribal territorial marker from pre- to post-Roman times.

There is much controversy over the original settlement date of Uttoxeter. Contemporary knowledge suggests that it was the Danes who settled the Heath area of the town around AD 600. Despite the fact that the name Uttoxeter has a Roman-looking spelling, it has actually evolved from around 70 different spelling variations.

Equally, there is no archaeological evidence to support either a Roman or Danish origin. The name for the Dove Valley at this time was the Celtic name 'Dubh', which can be roughly translated as 'dark water'; hence the valley was known as Dark Water Valley, or something similar.

From around AD 449, following the Roman departure from Britain, to around 580, the area saw Saxon invasion and settlement. Easily penetrating to the centre of Britain by the great rivers of the Trent, Humber and Ouse, the invaders came to settle in the rich grazing and farming lands of the river valleys. Uttoxeter and its surrounding area was born from the almost constant fighting between Saxons and Britons, between the Saxons themselves, and then between Saxons and Vikings. The area was close to the edge of the boundary of the Danelaw and Harold's eventual Saxon kingdom.

There is some evidence that the first church was built on the site of St Mary's Church in the market square around AD828, so it appears that the settlement nearest the Dove Valley was beginning to develop here around this time. Alfgar, Earl of Mercia (grandson of Lady Godiva) held the land here (along with much of the Midlands) before the time of the Norman invasion. His sons were later to revolt against William and the Norman invaders, who exacted bloody reprisals as a result.

The Domesday Book in 1086 records Uttoxeter as a modestly sized settlement of around 60 acres and possessing one slave. Much of Staffordshire rebelled against the Normans following the invasion, and vast parts were laid to waste. Very little remains of Norman and medieval Uttoxeter apart from the 14th-century tower of the parish church, but it was during this time that the Market Place took on its distinctive double square shape.

In 1252, Earl Ferrers granted a charter of various privileges including a market, and in 1308 the Earl of Lancaster granted a charter for a market every Wednesday, which is still held today. Trade grew alongside the market and fairs. Great craftsmen and artists flourished, such as Henry Yevele, 'England's finest architect', who worked under Chaucer on the nave of Westminster Abbey. Uttoxeter's tradition of nurturing great craftsmen continued: later, Robert Bakewell, born in 1682, became England's foremost wrought ironsmith.

During the civil wars of the 17th century, Uttoxeter was largely on the Parliamentary side, perhaps because Charles I had sold the town to speculators and a good proportion of common land was lost to the people. The town also saw the last surrender of the Royalist forces led by the Duke of Hamilton in 1646. Hamilton was interviewed by Cromwell himself, and eventually found guilty of treason and beheaded in 1649. In 1646, records show that the town was visited by the plague. In 1672, most of the lower part of the town was consumed by a fire.

In the 17th century the coaching age arrived; Uttoxeter found itself strategically located on a major route between Derby and Newcastle

MARKET PLACE *c1965* U29054

in northwest Staffordshire. The town became a minor coaching centre and a convenient staging post for coaches from Manchester en route to Birmingham and London.

The town equalled Stafford and Lichfield in its importance as a commercial centre from medieval times right through to the early 18th century. The first pots made in Stoke on Trent were used to transport butter to the town's markets. This 'Golden Age of Uttoxeter' was reflected in the number of trades which made the town famous: leather making, brewing, weaving, jewellery making, and later clock making.

Later still came the canal. At one time it was the terminus of the Caldon or Uttoxeter Canal. Little evidence of this remains; the 1811 canal warehouse was demolished despite local objections in 2004. The route was converted into the Churnet Valley Railway, which was opened in 1849. The railway linked Uttoxeter to the northwest, and made Uttoxeter an important railway junction. The railway helped the development of the dairy industry, which flourished at that time - milk trains travelled daily on to the south. The railway also provided a boost for the racecourse, which opened in 1908 on the Old Town Meadows next to the station.

Uttoxeter moved from the 19th century into the 20th with a sense of optimism. It was prosperous market town with a thriving livestock and other associated agricultural markets, and a plethora of related trades such as saddlery and tanning - some of the old workshops can still be seen around the town today. A good example is at the rear of the One Pound Shop (formerly Carters) in the market place. This building, the width of man with his arms outstretched, housed at least three saddlers until 1875, when it was acquired by the Carter family. They owned and operated it for at least 100 years; the shop, 'R Carter', was known well to all those wanting to purchase models, toys and hardware for many, many years until the owners' retirement.

Uttoxeter was also blessed with good communication routes. It was situated on the busy Derby to Crewe railway line, which is probably etched in the memory of many who lived in Uttoxeter; the regular sounds of half-mile-long heavy goods trains carrying anything from coal to cars would be heard throughout the town. A local saying on the Heath side of the town was that if you could hear the sound of the wheels of the train squeaking, it was a sure sign that it was going to rain!

The town also acquired a coal depot (which closed in the late 1970s). Thousands of tons of coal were heaped on an area south of the railway line by the road bridge over the line and stretching for hundreds of yards on the opposite side of the Hockley brook towards the Pinfold Crossing. This depot was no doubt the reason that many small local coal merchants grew and prospered before the advent of smokeless zones and an increasingly acute awareness of environmental issues. One such business which many will remember was Keelings. Based at a small yard on Ashbourne Road, Bill Keeling was a familiar face, black with coal dust and streaked with sweat, manually carrying 50-pound sacks of coal around the streets of Uttoxeter from his lorry to coal cellars.

The location of the town close to the railway, and in an agricultural area, no doubt also provided the necessary markets for Uttoxeter's many industrial entrepreneurs. Around 1845 Henry Bamford began producing agricultural equipment in Market Street. No 1 Market Street still bears a 'B' for Bamford, and the elaborate stonework of this corner building was commissioned by Henry Bamford, providing a monument to the family business. He also built the Oldfields cricket ground and pavilion (now a listed building) close to his home, Oldfields Hall, which is now a middle school on Bramshall Road.

Initially, Bamford's produced many different kinds of machines, dissimilar to the agricultural machines it made in its heyday. Early products included root cutters, water pumps, cheese cutters, and oil cake cutters, before the switch was made to the more familiar machinery related to the cultivation of the land. It was Samuel Bamford, Henry's son, who developed the business further around 1871 into a large factory to the south of the railway line: Leighton Ironworks stretched from Hockley Crossing to Bridge Street, around a quarter of a mile.

The works siren was a sound that invaded the lives of many in the town for years after the Second World War, whether they worked there or not! For decades it called the workforce to work, and sent them home again. Many will also remember the consequences of the siren's call, as a tide of hundreds of cloth-capped workers flowed down the streets of the town to converge at the works. The industry fell into decline in the eighties, and eventually closed. The factory remained empty before becoming the home of JCB heavy products a few years later.

JCB Excavators were linked to the Bamford agricultural equipment family. Joseph Bamford split from the family business after the war and began manufacturing trailers, allegedly in a shed by the site of Fryers Garage in Derby Road (this long established local business was demolished for housing in the early 1990s). The fledgling business grew into the well-known giant international excavator company JCB, which has three plants around Uttoxeter along with the Leighton Ironworks site, as well as many international locations.

Another industry which still dominates the town today is the local food industry - biscuits. Anyone visiting Uttoxeter may well mention the

MARKET PLACE *c1955* U29014

14

sweet and often mouth-watering smell of baking biscuits, which pervades the town several times a week. This business now occupies a large factory and is major local employer. The originator of the business was C H Elkes, whose name became an international brand name for biscuits - so much so, that despite the company's being acquired by other companies such as Adams Foods, Northern Foods and the recent merger with Fox's Biscuits, the brand names Elkes has often been retained. Elkes began his bakery business around 1908, and began making biscuits twenty years later. Today, the company trading under Fox's name, employs around 1600 people.

The wars hit Uttoxeter hard in terms of loss of life. In the First World War it was estimated that in one in thirty of all men from Uttoxeter died in the conflict. Uttoxeter's war memorial, positioned at the east end of the market place, was unveiled to commemorate their sacrifice in 1928; added to it are the names of those who died in the Second World War. Other names of those lost in wars, including recent conflicts, can be found on the wall of Trinity House, a listed building and part of Thomas Alleyne's High School. The war memorial and the church were illuminated in the 1990s after work by local man and personality Frank Parker, and now the giant 179-foot spire of St Mary's Parish Church can be seen for many miles at night.

The Second World War saw little direct action against Uttoxeter, although some bombing was directed at the town and at Leighton Ironworks. Anti-aircraft guns were situated in the cattle market car park, close to the great concrete blocks which still sit there. These blocks, around ten feet square, are actually the foundations for the great cranes of a large sawmill which flourished here in the 19th century.

From the Second World War on, Uttoxeter entered a period of stability and relative prosperity as a market town. Employment levels were as good as they are today, owing to the development of the A50 link road and its industrial corridor. As the town entered the seventies, gradual decline began to set in; the market town lost major employers, and general economic depression had its effect. The biggest blow came as its livestock market began to slow down, and with the market's eventual loss to property speculators. The core of the town had gone. Other markets suffered, and so did the general retail markets; Uttoxeter lost its market day hustle, bustle and vitality.

The area's development plans of 1991 did nothing to help the situation, for they provided little land for economic development and a general free-for-all in terms of housing. Giant estates subsequently grew at the Parks and Westlands Road - known locally as 'Birdland', owing to the developers' somewhat unimaginative naming of the roads - and the die was cast for the town's future as a dormitory town serving local cities.

Uttoxeter is now rapidly becoming a dormitory town for commuters to the cities of Stoke on Trent, Nottingham and Derby, though hope remains for its regeneration and economic revival through the Market Towns Initiative. What endures at its core is the ancient heart of a town which in its own way tells the story of the people of the British Isles through the centuries.

UTTOXETER *from the air 1975* AFA29557

UTTOXETER LIVING MEMORIES

DOVE BRIDGE *c1955* U29022

In 1642 Charles I was confronted on the approach to the bridge by a contingent of Staffordshire residents asking him to come to terms with Parliament. He ignored their pleas. The new A50 bypass has meant that the bridge is now an attractive stop on the Staffordshire Way.

◄ THE OLD TALBOT INN *c1955*
U29009A

The Old Talbot was built in 1527, and is reputed to be the oldest building in Uttoxeter. It survived two fires which badly damaged the town in 1596 and 1672. The coat of arms on the inn sign depicts its name: a talbot, or hound, was the crest of the Talbots, Earls of Shrewsbury. Recent renovations have revealed more of the timber-framed structure.

◀ LATHROPP'S ALMSHOUSES
c1955 U29016

In 1700 William Lathropp built these almshouses for poor widows. Thomas Fradgley refurbished them in 1848 at a cost of £300. Some residents have complained of feeling a cold presence, and of a smell of leather. At one time there used to be a tannery in existence on the site.

▲ THE CATTLE MARKET *c1965* U29077

The Smithfield Market opened in 1854, costing £1500 to build; it was situated at the rear of the Town Hall. The stalls could contain up to 800 head of cattle, 840 sheep and 220 pigs. The market will move to new premises in 2005.

◀ detail from U29077

DR JOHNSON'S MEMORIAL *c1955* U29008

The Kiosk was originally erected as the market superintendent's office in 1854, and once functioned as a weighing machine. In 1877 the bas-relief depicting Dr Johnson's penance was added (in later life, Johnson set himself the penance of standing at the Uttoxeter market on the spot where his father had his stall. This was to expiate his disobedience of years before in refusing to help his father there). In 1987 an ancient well was discovered by council workmen directly underneath the kiosk during repairs to a manhole in front of it.

THE MARKET PLACE
c1965 U29054

Here we see the kiosk being used as a traffic roundabout. The lantern atop the building has now gone. Here the view of the kiosk is all but obliterated by a telephone exchange box, a police telephone box and the large road sign which gives directions to Stoke, Stafford, Rugeley and the Uttoxeter Lido. These have all since been removed.

THE PARK *c1965* U29095

This area is still known as the Wharf to locals, despite being officially renamed Park Place in 1911 to celebrate the coronation of George V. The Uttoxeter branch of the 13-mile Trent & Mersey Canal (or Caldon Canal) terminated at the rear of the houses here from 1811 to 1847. The railway arrived in 1847, and the canal was closed. It quickly became the site of the North Staffordshire Railway Company line, until that in turn closed under Dr Beeching in 1965. It is ironic that the Trent & Mersey Canal is now one of the country's most popular canal routes, and there is talk again of re-opening the Uttoxeter stretch. The shop on the left is J T Walker's bakery and confectioner's shop, previously owned by Mr Collis in 1906.

THE WAR MEMORIAL
c1965 U29051

The war memorial was unveiled by Colonel Ratcliffe of the North Staffordshire Regiment. The National Inventory of War Memorials has estimated the number of war memorials in the UK to be between 50,000 to 60,000. War memorials tell us much about a town; many of the family names are still familiar in the area, and are often heartbreakingly repeated in subsequent wars. Every year on Armistice Day a wreath-laying parade and service is held here.

THE WAR MEMORIAL AND THE CHURCH
c1955 U29032

The war memorial was funded by public subscription and unveiled on 11 November 1928, 10 years to the day after the Armistice of the First World War. The octagonal monument was carved by Robert Bridgman & Sons of Lichfield. A high proportion of men from Uttoxeter were killed during the war, 177 out of a population of 5,717, according to the 1911 census.

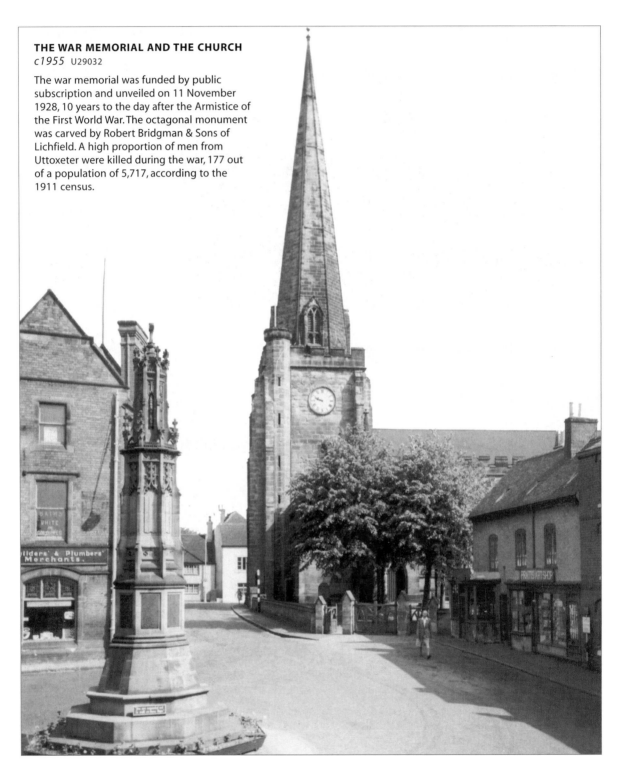

THE WAR MEMORIAL
c1955 U29006

The original White Horse pub can be seen behind the war memorial; it was demolished to make way for the incongruous new 1960s town planning building. The new White Horse was itself seriously damaged by fire in 2004, when the roof and much of the upper floor were badly affected. The original White Horse Inn was built in 1830 and owned by John Twigg; there were 24 pubs in Uttoxeter at that time. An ancient market cross with 24 steps once stood at this site.

THE MARKET PLACE *c1965* U29089

From left to right the shops are J Phillips & Sons, plumbers and decorators, established in 1836; the Old Talbot Inn, built in 1527; the Provincial Building Society; the Co-operative furniture department; Wilks, ladies' outfitters; and the Liquor Vaults public house. Notice the bus stop road markings outside Wilks's shop - there was no bus station in the town at this time.

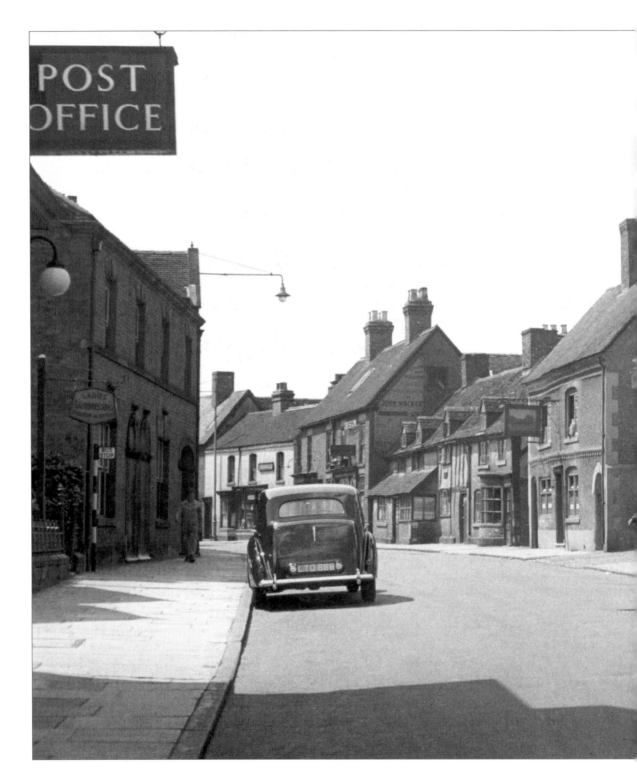

CARTER STREET
c1955 U29002

The White Hart Hotel (right) was once the headquarters for the Automobile Club of Great Britain. In 1745, supporters of Bonnie Prince Charlie used the White Hart Hotel as their headquarters, and their ringleader Sir William Bagot was arrested there. The Coach & Horses Inn next to the White Hart Hotel were used as a bar for the White Hart Hotel before it closed down.

THE MARKET PLACE
c1955 U29029

On the left, the buildings are Maypole, a grocery shop, once the site of the Crown public house (the rear of the yard is still known as Crown Yard) and the Westminster Bank before it became the Nat West in 1968. In the centre distance are the White Horse Inn and Whieldon's Green Bus depot, which became Stevenson's. The Vine Inn, a Truefit shoe shop, Pakeman & Co, grocers, and Bradley's men's outfitters are on the right.

HIGH STREET
c1955 U29003

The High Street leads to the Market Place. In the foreground is Boots the Chemist; Boots took over the shop from Thomas Woolrich, a chemist and druggist, in 1921. The building has since been rebuilt, but it is still home to Boots. Next door is Geo. Orme & Sons Ltd, selling clothing. The Ormes had a number of outlets in the town. Bradley's (men's outfitters), Wadham (ladies' outfitters), and George Mason (grocers) are on the far right. Also notice the street light which hangs suspended across the street.

HIGH STREET *c1955*
U29004

The Cross Keys Inn on the left is now Bagshaws, an estate agent's; the upper floors were converted into apartments in 2004. The timber-framed Town Hall keeper's house beyond was demolished in 1970 for the Fine Fare supermarket (now Wilkinsons). The lorry loaded with milk churns would have collected them from United Dairies Ltd, which was situated near the railway station. Millions of gallons of milk were sent out across the country from the rich grazing lands of the Dove and Churnet valleys.

**MARKET PLACE AND
HIGH STREET** *c1955*
U29031

On the left is the Old Talbot
Inn, rumoured to be the
oldest existing building
in the town. Before the
sending of condemned men
to Stafford for execution,
the grisly deed was
undertaken in the yard at
the rear of this pub, and
the prisoners were held
in its cellars. The Leek &
Moorlands Building Society
next door became the Leek
& Westbourne Building
Society in 1965. Beyond is
the Co-Operative Society
before its move to new
premises in Carter Street,
and Salter & Salter, tailors.
The awning on the opposite
side of the street belongs to
W H Smith, the newsagents.

▶ **OLDFIELDS HALL SCHOOL** *c1965* U29070

The building dates from the late 1700s, and was originally called Oldfields House. In the 19th century it became Martha Bennett's school, before being bought by Charles Ford to be used as a house. It finally became the home of Mr John Bamford, eldest son of Captain Oswald Bamford, before its conversion again to a girls' secondary school in 1959. The school has been a 9-13 Middle School since 1974, and sits in the beautiful landscaped grounds of the original house.

◄ **HIGH STREET**
c1965 U29058

In the middle distance on the left are Bagshaws, estate agents in the town since 1871. Opposite is Woolworths, and then come the District Bank, T H Deville & Sons, butchers, and Dorothy Perkins, ladies' outfitters. In 1978 the shop closed after 30 years trading; its lease was sold to Greenwoods menswear store.

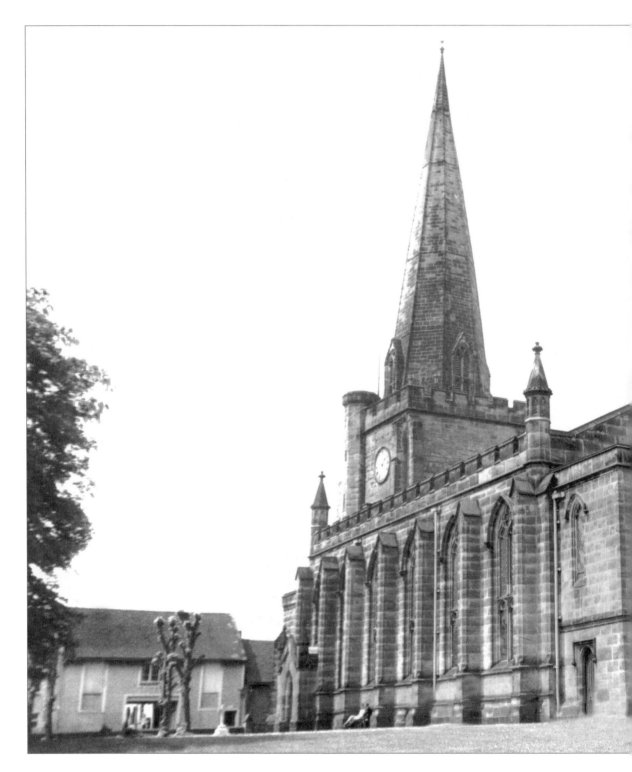

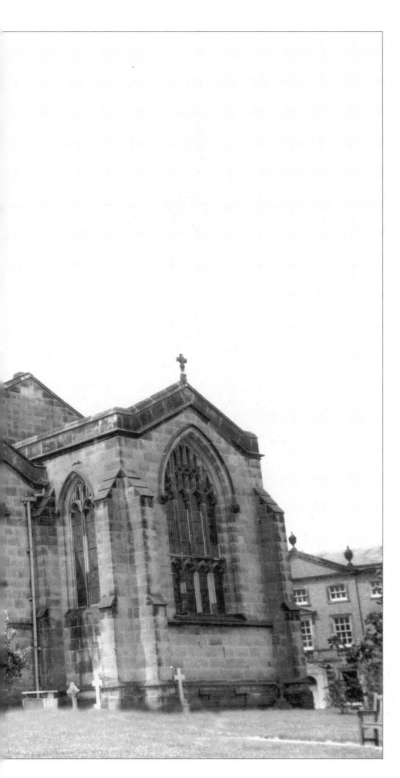

ST MARY'S PARISH CHURCH
c1955 U29097

The church tower dates back to 1327, and
was probably built by Henry Yevele and
his mason father. Henry went on to work
under Chaucer in designing the nave in
Westminster Abbey, and became
King Edward III's Master of the King's Works.

▲ **THE HOCKLEY** *c1955* U29037

The Hockley brook was a haven for the local children, as there was no swimming pool in Uttoxeter. The brook ran through land owned by Mr John Bamford of Oldfields Hall, who did not object to the children using it.

▶ *detail from* U29037

▲ **THE HOCKLEY BROOK** *c1955* U29038

This view of the Hockley brook was taken looking towards the town. An open-air swimming pool, the Lido, eventually arrived in 1964. The Hockley is home to several species of fish, including the barbel.

◀ *detail from* U29038

43

THE RACECOURSE
c1955 U29100

In 1908 a new racecourse
for National Hunt racing
was opened near Uttoxeter
railway station. Previously
there was a racecourse at
Lambert's Park Farm, near
Byrds Lane, and before
that on land opposite the
Butchers Arms Inn
at Bramshall.

▶ **THE LIDO** *c1965* U29093

Uttoxeter's open-air swimming pool was built in 1964; at first its use was seasonal. It underwent a large refurbishment in 1985 to include a leisure centre, and the pool was redesigned as an indoor heated facility.

◀ **THE LIDO**

c1965 U29065

The leisure centre was built over the existing swimming pool known as Uttoxeter Lido; the flag bears its name. The new centre was opened in 1985 by Olympic gold medallist David Wilkie.

MARKET PLACE *c1955*
U29015

On the left is Allport & Sons, a jeweller's, and next to it Mellor, a chemist's - behind its brick façade lies an Elizabethan jettied building. Over the square sits Stewart's, a butcher's, the Vine Inn, and a Truefit shoe shop. The coal lorry belonged to Eckersley Brothers, coal merchants, whose business was run from railway sidings on Bridge Street.

49

▲ **CARTER STREET** *c1955* U29001

The house on the left is now the Heritage Centre, once the home of Francis Redfern, the local historian (1851-1895). Redfern published two editions of 'The History and Antiquities of Uttoxeter'; the first edition was in 1865, and it was followed by a rewritten and enlarged edition in 1886. The Town Council purchased the building in 1987 and refurbished it as a Heritage Centre. Next to it was the Coach & Horses Inn, which closed its doors in the late 1950s. In the early 19th century the White Hart Hotel (beyond) was the town's main coaching inn. The horse and cart (right) was most likely to have belonged to the Co-operative Society.

▶ *detail from* U29001

THE MARKET *c1965* U29080

King Henry III gave exclusive rights to hold a Wednesday market, and granted a charter to the town in 1251. It was discovered in 2004 that the town had 'lost' this historic charter. After searching the public record office in Kew, the Uttoxeter Archaeological Society located the original document. This photograph was taken in the days when Uttoxeter had a much larger market. In addition to the Wednesday market, a Saturday market was established on 2 January 1904; it was opened by the Chairman of the Uttoxeter Urban Council, Mr A C Bunting, Esq, JP, CC. At 6 o'clock in the evening a grand torchlight procession took place, accompanied by the music of a brass band.

BLITHFIELD RESERVOIR *c1955* U29033

The 3,700 feet dam was constructed to hold four million gallons of water at a depth of 47 feet covering more than two miles. Work started in 1948, and the reservoir was officially opened by the Queen Mother in 1953. It quickly became an important habitat for water birds, and is now designated a site of special scientific interest.

HIGH STREET
c1955 U29013

Vehicles were allowed to enter the High Street from the narrow road next to Williams Deacon's Bank. With the building of the Maltings shopping centre and car park the road was closed to all traffic. Williams Deacon's Bank on the corner was built around 1920; it replaced Bell & Dams, a clock making and jewellery business established in the 18th century.

▼ THE GIRLS' HIGH SCHOOL *c1955* U29019

The Staffordshire Education Authority acquired the Hall on Dove Bank in 1919 and named it Uttoxeter Girls' High School. The building on the right is Thomas Alleyne's Grammar School, originally a school for boys. In 1974 the two schools became a single comprehensive, and it was renamed as Thomas Alleyne's High School.

▶ ALLEYNE'S GRAMMAR SCHOOL *c1955* U29020

The school was founded in 1558 in the will of Thomas Alleyne, a priest and Oxford scholar who was born in Uttoxeter. Queen Mary died in 1558, and Elizabeth I ascended the throne in November of that year. The school was originally on Bridge Street. It moved here to these new buildings on Derby Road (now called Back Lane) in 1859, having outgrown the original premises. In 1921 it became a maintained secondary school, and became a comprehensive in 1974.

◄ MARKET PLACE
c1965 U29059

There was no bus station in the town, so buses parked in designated ranks painted on the road surface. The red PMT (Potteries Motor Traction) buses on the left ran to Derby, and the buses on the right ran to Hanley. 1946 saw the first double-decker buses in Uttoxeter. Stevenson's Yellow Buses first ran from Uttoxeter to Burton on 11 September 1926. Whieldon's Green Bus Service ran buses from Uttoxeter to Stafford.

► PICKNALLS SCHOOL *c1965*
U29068

This school, situated in the south west of the town, takes its name from the brook which flows beside the Crewe-Derby railway line at the foot of the hill. The school was officially opened as a primary school in 1968, and then reorganised as a first school in 1974. The school currently has about 290 children, and has a very active Junior Archaeology Club. A beautiful Bronze Age axe was discovered in the grounds where the school now stands, and is on display in the Potteries Museum in Hanley, Stoke on Trent.

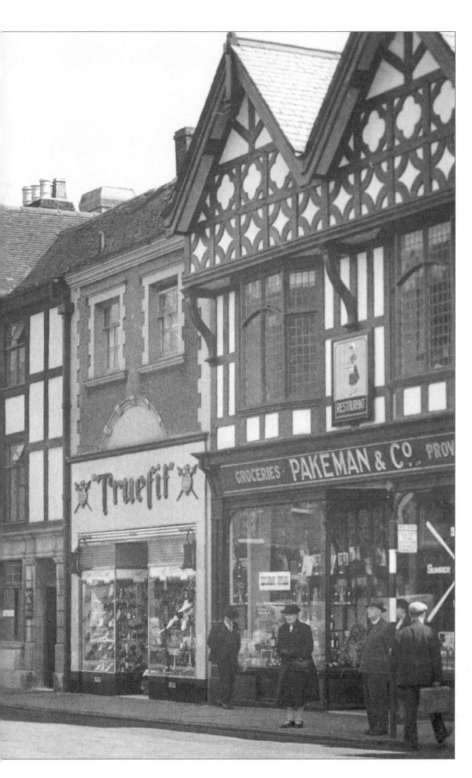

MARKET PLACE *c1955*
U29011

The building to the left of Truefit, the shoe shop, was called the Vine Inn; it commanded a clear view of the Market Place. In 1878 it was entirely rebuilt as a new public house called the Nags Head. It is now the Leek United Building Society.

▲ **MARKET PLACE** *c1965* U29053

Apart from automobile design, the view has hardly changed to this day. This area forms the second square of the market place and was once known as Bear Hill; this is believed to be the site where bear baiting took place. A bear or bull was tied to a stake and attacked by one or more dogs. The animal was sometimes made more ferocious by having pepper blown up its nostrils. The bear took vicious revenge on the onlookers if it managed to pull free - as sometimes happened!

▶ **AUSTIN A55 VAN** *c1965* U29053X

Parked outside J Cope & Son, a butcher's, is a classic Austin A55 van. This ½-ton sturdy commercial vehicle was reputedly a very comfortable drive. These vans are now collectable and extremely rare; a model was for sale on eBay, the internet auction site, at the time of writing.

HOCKLEY BROOK *c1965* U29094

The brook is named after the hamlet of Hockley a quarter of a mile south of the town centre - the hamlet is now subsumed into the town. Also known as the Picknalls Brook, the stream was used for many years in the industrial process of the Leighton or Bamford's ironworks. The newly planted trees seen here are now mature specimens screening the route of the railway line to Stoke and Derby.

59

THE LIDO *c1965* U29091

The diving pool was 12 feet 6 inches in depth, which is just as well, as the top board stood 15 feet in height. The name 'lido' is derived from the name of a place in Venice where bathing took place. Lidos usually have areas for sunbathing, watching, and eating, and are designed for activities around the water. The 1930s saw a big rise in outdoor swimming, but many pools closed in the 1970s, sad to say. There are now only around 70 outdoor lidos in the UK.

MARKET PLACE *c1965* U29088

Behind the Georgian and Victorian façades of many of these buildings lie the timber frameworks of 15th- and 16th-century houses. Older residents of the town can still recall some of the brick facades being erected over the original frontages. This activity would now be outlawed under listed building legislation, which was introduced in 1947. The act ensured that all surviving buildings built before 1700 and most buildings built between 1700 and 1840 would be listed if they had not been too much altered.

MARKET PLACE *c1965* U29087

Taken on the same day as No U29088, this photograph shows a busy Market Place and High Street scene. An illegally parked 1960s estate car misses (for now) the attention of the traffic policeman outside the kiosk. 50mph speed limits were introduced on trunk roads in 1965 in an effort to reduce road accidents. Stop signs were introduced, and all new cars from 1 September had to have flashing turn indicators; brake stop lights were also made compulsory.

MARKET PLACE *c1965*
U29086

This street scene shows the Provincial Building Society and the Co-operative Society; across the road is an impressive crescent of shops with offices and apartments above. It is believed that the crescent may have been designed by Thomas Gardner of Uttoxeter. Gardner was the son of a carpenter, and was trained in that trade. Like many carpenters in the mid 18th century, he swiftly moved on to become a builder. He trained under Joseph Pickford of Derby.

THE MARKET *c1965* U29084

In this market scene, the farm machinery for sale on the shop forecourt and pavement demonstrate the abiding association of the town with the rich agricultural heritage of the area. Uttoxeter's role as a local centre of agriculture and trade saw the birth of two major enterprises, Elkes Biscuits, known for its Malted Milk variety, and JCB, one of the world's largest manufacturers of earthmoving, agricultural and materials handling equipment. Both of these companies are still major contributors to the local economy.

▲ **THE MARKET** *c1965* U29083

The chimney stack in the background formed part of the Bamford Leighton Ironworks, which was established in 1871 and covered 24 acres. The foundry, an addition to the ironmongery business established by Henry Bamford in 1845, allowed the firm to expand. The firm was a family partnership until 1916, when it became a private limited company.

◀ *detail from* U29083

THE MARKET *c1965* U29082

Today the imposing Georgian doorway which can be seen to the left of the market stalls has been lost, to be replaced by garish shop fronts. In the centre of the photograph we can see the 16th-century Tudor buildings of Sargeant's, a butcher's, before their splendid sympathetic restoration in 1980.

THE MARKET *c1965* U29081

We are looking north across the Market Place. The distinctive van belonged to Robirch Pies of Burton on Trent. The market supplied many of the town's needs from local food produce and clothing to crockery and books for centuries before the arrival of convenience stores and supermarkets.

THE CATTLE MARKET
c1965 U29078

Before the cattle market was built in Smithfield, cattle were sold in the Market Place, sheep by the Black Swan pub, pigs on Bear Hill and horses in Balance Street. In effect, the whole town centre became the market. Residents remember travelling into town by horse and cart from the local farms for market day even in the 20th century.

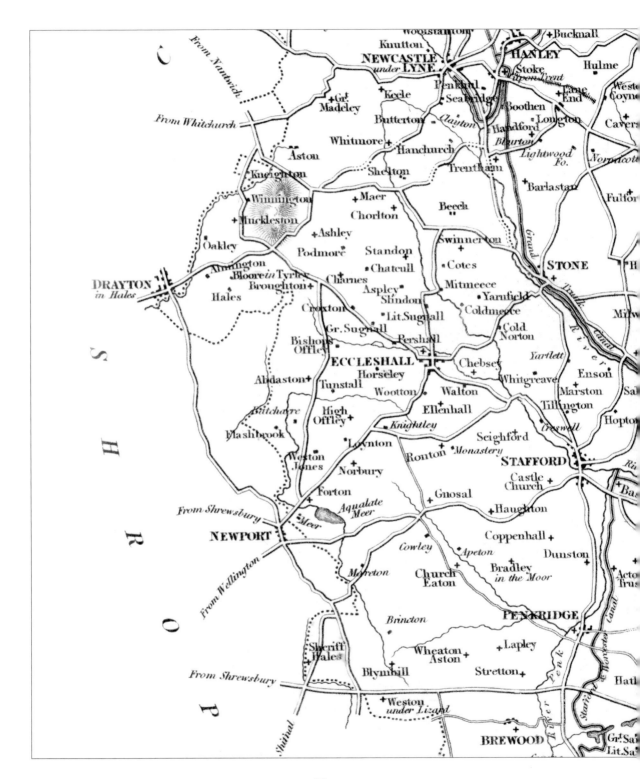

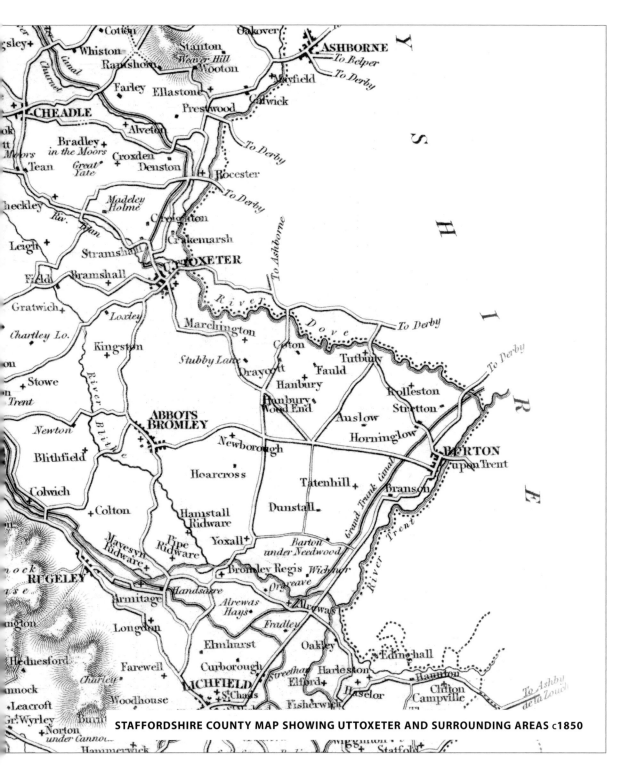

STAFFORDSHIRE COUNTY MAP SHOWING UTTOXETER AND SURROUNDING AREAS c1850

▶ **THE CATTLE MARKET**
c1965 U29076

Just two years after this photograph was taken, foot and mouth disease devastated the industry. The 1967 outbreak was still remembered by many when the 2001 crisis hit hard. It was in November 1967 when the foot and mouth crisis hit its peak, though the media were not as preoccupied with reporting it as they were in 2001. In 1967, the papers were too concerned with the devaluation of the pound and conflicts in Aden and Vietnam.

◀ THE CATTLE MARKET
c1965 U29075

Uttoxeter cattle market was the biggest market south of Nantwich. Before the foot and mouth outbreak of 2001, it hosted fat and store cattle sales on Mondays, Wednesdays and Saturdays. Since the outbreak it now only sells on Wednesdays. It is still the venue for the UK's largest sale of Holsteins. The Holstein breed originated in the Netherlands close to 2,000 years ago. The black cows and white cows of the Batavians and Friesians were bred and culled to produce cows that made the best use of limited land by producing the most milk. Eventually these animals evolved genetically into the efficient, high-producing black and white dairy cows known as the Holstein-Friesian.

THE CHURCH *c1965* U29062

We are looking west across the churchyard. The ancient headstones were lifted and placed against the boundary wall and used to cover the retaining walls with steps. Though this was not an uncommon practice, it has rendered many of the stones unreadable through wear.

THE CHURCH *c1965* U29061

This view shows the 14th-century tower and spire of St Mary's Church. The spire rises to a height of 179 feet; it was hit by lightning in 1814, and had to be partly rebuilt. The Wheatsheaf and the White Horse public houses can be seen on the right. Debate still rages about the dedication of the church: is it to St Mary the Virgin or St Mary Magdalene? The nave and chancel of St Mary's was rebuilt in 1828 at a cost of £6,061 1s 1ld. The building work revealed evidence that the church stood on a much older building, possibly of the 7th or 8th century. The tower and steeple date to the late 12th century, and is believed to be the work of Roger de Yevele and his son Henry Yevele, who has been described as 'the greatest English architect'. Henry was probably born in Uttoxeter between 1320 and 1330, and some of the work on the church may be his own. Yevele knew Chaucer and worked under him on the nave of Westminster Abbey. He went on to work on Durham Cathedral, Old St Paul's and the Bloody Tower.

▼ **MARKET PLACE** *c1965* U29060

No parking restrictions were in place at this date, and the Market Place served as the bus station. Car ownership was still a minority activity, despite the number of cars we can see here. The High Street served as the main thoroughfare until the bypass, first mooted before the war, was eventually built. On the right is the Milk Bar where you could buy exotic ice creams, with Mellor's the optician's next door and Edward Martin's the jeweller's next to that; these buildings are now a pizza place, an estate agent's and an off licence respectively.

► **CARTER STREET AND THE WHITE HART** *c1965*
U29057

The White Hart dates back to the 17th century. Supporters of Bonnie Prince Charlie used the inn as their headquarters in 1745. In 2004 it was the scene of the first ever trial to take place in a pub. A temporary courtroom was set up in the White Hart when a claimant could not travel owing to illness.

◀ MARKET PLACE c1965
U29056

In 1965, the Beatles' 'Help!' was released, and mini mania was taking hold. We can see the Leek and Westbourne Building Society, the Co-op, and the gas showroom on the left, and further along Barclays Bank stands next to the 17th-century Cross Keys Inn, home of Bagshaws, the auctioneers, surveyors, and estate agents. Bagshaws was founded in 1871 by Thomas Beardmore, the landlord of the Three Tuns in Uttoxeter. By 1886 he had joined forces with W S Bagshaw, a local coal merchant, and the firm became Beardmore & Bagshaw. By the early 1890s, W S Bagshaw was the sole proprietor.

▶ MARKET PLACE
c1965 U29055

By 1965 the car was increasingly making its impact on Uttoxeter, as we can see from the number of parked cars. The large Maltings car park which exists today was at the time being cleared for the bus station - it was once the site of Bunting's Brewery. Bunting's once owned many pubs in the area, and distributed its ales far and wide. It went out of business in the 1930s, and its buildings were demolished in the early 1960s, at the time this picture was taken.

▼ **HIGH STREET** *c1955* U29009

This scene shows a traffic-free view along the High Street. Once known as Old Street, this has been the main road through the town for centuries. Carnival parades were annual events until recently, and visiting circus entertainers along with their animals used to parade the length of the street advertising their shows. The building on the corner with the clock showing 2.20 (right) is Williams Deacon's Bank. This was the name the Royal Bank of Scotland were trading under from 1920; it became Williams & Glyns Bank before returning to its original name in 1985. The bank itself was founded in 1727. Thomas Hart established the first bank in Uttoxeter in the 18th century at the Bank House; the original safe can still be seen in situ today. The Bank House was designed by Thomas Gardner of Uttoxeter, and is in fact a simpler copy of Joseph Pickford's house (now a museum) in Derby.

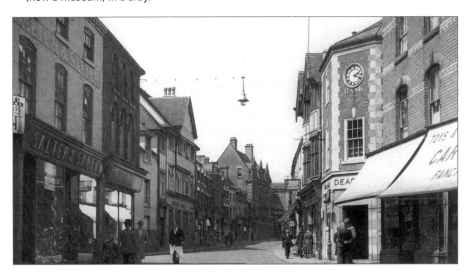

▶ **THE CHURCH** *c1955*
U29025

This view was taken from the war memorial. The cottages to the right were at this time home and shop to H Woolley, a saddler, as they had been since around 1900. The cottages date from the 16th century, and are probably of the same age as the earliest known parish register of 1596. Notice the old Whieldon's green bus parked outside.

◄ **MARKET PLACE**
c1955 U29014

Alternatively known as Johnson's Memorial, the kiosk or the conduit is now arguably one of the smallest newsagents in the world. A conduit has existed here for centuries to channel underground springs for use by the people of the town. The original pedestal lantern on the top of the conduit was replaced in the early 1960s with an incongruous double headed lantern – we may be thankful that it was subsequently removed. A new lantern is planned, based on the original, which will be more in keeping with the neo-classical building of 1854.

▶ **HIGH STREET**
c1960 U29040

Gazing up the street past Wilks Teenage Fashions (left) with the Elkes Cafe above, we can see Barclays Bank. This was built in 1921 on the site of Huggins & Chambers, an ironmonger's. The ironmonger's sold Witchem's firelighters among other products - these must have contributed to the conflagration when the building was burned to the ground in 1920.

HIGH STREET *c1955*
U29005

A classic Ford car stands on the left beside Woolworths. The first Woolworths in the UK, a subsidiary of the US firm, opened in Liverpool in 1909, and branches spread rapidly throughout the country. The man in the centre of the photograph is a chimney sweep carrying rods on his back. Whilst food rationing introduced during the war ended in 1954, coal rationing did not end until 1958, so the sweep would have been much busier after this date. The war saw troops from as far afield as Poland, Belgium and the USA stationed in the area. In 1940 jettisoned bombs landed at the end of New Road, though no one was hurt.

HOLLY ROAD ESTATE *c1965* U29072

Here we see new building in what is now Hall Road. There was
a great building expansion of building in the 1960s in Uttoxeter
of both private and council housing. In the 1960s, about 400,000
homes were built in Britain each year, and more than half of
these were council houses. Local authority house building has
now disappeared, and housing associations build about 15,000
homes a year.

THE GIRLS' HIGH SCHOOL *c1955* U29018

This photograph of the Girls' High School shows the tennis courts in front of the main brick building. During the coal strikes of 1973/74 there was not enough coal to heat the boys' school, so older boys were sent to the girls' school. During breaks the boys were herded into the tennis courts to separate them from the girls.

MARKET PLACE *c1955*
U29036

A ceremony is held here each year on the nearest Monday to Johnson's birthday on 18 September; speeches are made, and a laurel wreath is laid at the foot of the monument. The window was added in the 1920s or 1930s. A Pakeman & Son's delivery van can be seen in the centre of the photograph. Pakeman & Son was one of the many grocers in the town; the shop stands to the right of the Truefit shoe shop. Shoppers had a personal relationship with shopkeepers, and shops were places of gossip and information. It has been estimated that there were between 60,000 and 90,000 grocers' shops in the UK in the late 1940s; this was soon to change following the introduction of self-service shopping and supermarkets.

MARKET PLACE *c1955*
U29012x

The kiosk is advertising Morin's ice cream. Uttoxeter is more well-known for Ashmore's ice cream, a speciality of the town. The firm was founded in 1932. During the Second World War, Ashmore's made ice cream only for the American troops stationed in Sudbury, as the delicacy was not available owing to rationing. As there was no bus station, PMT buses are parked up here for the next service. The waiting drivers share a chat and smile for the photographer.

BRAMSHALL ROAD RECREATION GROUND
c1965 U29073

In 1921 Uttoxeter Urban District Council set up a committee to provide a recreation ground. Mr C H Elkes, a local businessman, offered an eleven-acre field sloping down to the Picknall or Hockley Brook. The recreation ground was opened in 1925. In 1953 festivities were held here to celebrate Queen Elizabeth's coronation. It is used regularly today for sporting activities, and creates a green avenue through the town to the Hockley Bridge.

BAMFORD'S SPORTS GROUND *c1965* U29069

Uttoxeter had the first recorded cricket club in the country. In 1904 John Bamford's love of cricket inspired him to purchase a field opposite his home on Bramshall Road. He built a pavilion, and invited such famous cricket players as W G Grace, Hobbs, Hardstaff, and Rhodes here. Early in the 20th century the ground was home to many first-class matches with teams from Australia and South Africa. The sports ground has been home to Uttoxeter Rugby Football Club since 1982.

INDEX

Alleyne's Grammar School 54

Bamford's Sports Ground 88

Blithfield Reservoir 51

Bramshall Road Recreation Ground 88

Carter Street 28-29, 50, 76

Cattle Market 21, 68-69, 72-73

Dove Bridge 18-19

Dr Johnson's Memorial 22

Girls' High School 54, 83

High Street 10, 32-33, 34-35, 36-37, 38-39, 52-53, 78, 79, 80-81, 82

Hockley 42, 43

Hockley Brook 59

Holly Road Estate 82

Lathropp's Almshouses 20-21

Lido 46-47, 60

Market Place 12, 14, 23, 27, 30-31, 36-37, 48-49, 51, 55, 56-57, 58, 61, 62-63, 64, 65, 66, 67, 76, 77, 79, 84-85, 86-87

Old Houses

Old Talbot Inn 20

Oldfields Hall School 38-39

Park 23

Picknalls School 55

Racecourse 44-45

St Mary's Parish Church 26, 40-41, 74, 75, 78

War Memorial 24-25, 26, 27

White Hart 76

NAMES OF SUBSCRIBERS

The following people have kindly supported this book by subscribing to copies before publication.

Susan & Malcolm Ainsworth, Cheadle, Staffs
The Allen Family, Uttoxeter
The Allen Family of Uttoxeter (2005)
Mr & Mrs B C Barton, Uttoxeter
The Bartram Family, Uttoxeter
John Beeson and sons, Kingstone
Mr L Bellamy & Mrs S Bellamy &
    Mr A Stubbs
Mr E W & Mrs C A Bettany, Uttoxeter
In loving memory of Joyce Blomeley
David L Bowd, Zeta, Lee & Lisa, Rocester
Pat & Vin Bradley, Uttoxeter
Brian, Joan & Alan Brewer, Uttoxeter
Lynda Frances Brindley
D W Brough, Uttoxeter
Andy & Gail Bryan, Uttoxeter
Les & Helen Buckely, Marchington
Mr S P & Mrs J A Burgess & Sami,
    Uttoxeter
Ann Burton, Uttoxeter
Jean Burton, Uttoxeter
To Butch on your 65th, with love Cynthia
The Capewell Family
The Capewell Family, Nr Uttoxeter
In memory of W H Capewell, Uttoxeter
The Carter Family, Hatton
Daniel Carter, moved here Jan 2003
The Chatfield Family, Uttoxeter
Kevin & Christine Colclough
The Crane Family, Uttoxeter
The Crosby Family, Stramshall
David, Donna, Sam & Lauren Crutchley
The Darby's of Uttoxeter
Tim Dawson of Denstone & Family

Gladys Noreen Denny - Thanks! David
In memory of the Ducie & Tate Families
In memory of Chris Ede of Waterloo Farm
Tribute to my family, Joan Ede, Uttoxeter
In memory of Chris Egerton
The Emery Family, Gratwich, Uttoxeter
For my parents, Colin & Phyllis Eyre,
    Uttoxeter
Mr & Mrs K Fallows, Happy Wedding
    Anniversary
To Lily Fallows with love Sue Wildsmith
The Flanaghan Family of Uttoxeter
Frederick Ernest Ford
Maurice Ford, Uttoxeter
Evenlyn Lucy Fountain, Uttoxeter
Michael Fox, Church Broughton
Jean Glover, Barking, Essex
To my Dad, Chris Goodall, Tean S-O-T
In memory of Michael Groombridge
To Hilda Hanks on her 100th Birthday
Betty, Ralph & Petra Harris and Joshua
    & Matthew Handy
Anne Harrison, Uttoxeter
The Herbert Family
Mr & Mrs B Herrod, Ella & Jacob, Uttoxeter
The Higgs Family, Uttoxeter
The Hobbs Family, Kingstone
Janet Howes
Michael Joseph Johnson
David Jones, Uttoxeter (formerly Rocester)
Rev P & Mrs T Jones, Uttoxeter
The Kent Family, Bramshall
Harriet Langridge
Steve & Jackie Lavin, Uttoxeter

In memory of Clive Leech, Uttoxeter
Ann & Sandy Liddle, Marchington
Robert Liddle, Hanbury
For Alice Lowe and in memory of Tom Lowe
M Milner, Uttoxeter
Margaret & Michael Mitchell, May 2005
In memory of Donald Edward Morris
Sheila & Ron Morris, Hall Road, Uttoxeter
Mr Bernard Mycock, Uttoxeter
The Nash Family of Uttoxeter
Lionel & Barbara Nash, & Heather,
    Peter & Colin
To my parents love Carol Oakes & Family,
    Uttoxeter
Jean M Owen
The Owen Family, Uttoxeter
In memory of Ronald Parker, Uttoxeter
G & N Peach, in memory of A & G Bates
The Phillips Family, Blounts Green Farm
Mr Peter & Mrs Teresa Phillips, Uttoxeter
Picknalls First School, Uttoxeter
G I Plant, Uttoxeter, Happy Christmas Mum
In memory of H J Porter, Marchington
Geoffrey Harold Potter
Bruce & Jane Punchard, Uttoxeter
The Punchard Family, Uttoxeter
Mr David Quick & Mrs Peggy Quick
James G A Ratcliffe, with memories of
    Uttoxeter
Peter & Margaret Rock, Golden Wedding,
    Aug 2005
In memory of Fred Sanbrooke, Uttoxeter
Rosemary Sault, Yoxall
The Simpson Family, Uttoxeter

George T Smith and Family, Uttoxeter
Mr G R Smith, Uttoxeter
Gwen Smith, as a thank you, David
Kay Smith
Michael A Smith, Uttoxeter
Ray Smith, Uttoxeter
Philip G Stubbs
Mr V K & Mrs A C Sunley, Uttoxeter
The Underhill Family, Uttoxeter
Uttoxeter Post & Times
In memory of Fred & Dorothy Wagstaff
A tribute to my parents,
    Mr & Mrs Fred Wagstaffe
Mick Wainwright and Julie Beardmore 2005
The Walker Family, Uttoxeter
John, Laura & Bethany Walton, Uttoxeter
The Weir Family, Uttoxeter
G T Wells, Uttoxeter,
    Happy Birthday Mum x
Roddy & Sheila Whiston, Uttoxeter
The Whites to The Balls, Shipton Drive
O I Whittingham
C Williams & Family, Uttoxeter
The Wilson Family of Spiceal St, Uttoxeter
J V & E M Woodward & Family, Uttoxeter
The Wyche Family, Uttoxeter

FRITH PRODUCTS & SERVICES

Francis Frith would doubtless be pleased to know that the pioneering publishing venture he started in 1860 still continues today. Over a hundred and forty years later, The Francis Frith Collection continues in the same innovative tradition and is now one of the foremost publishers of vintage photographs in the world. Some of the current activities include:

Interior Decoration

Today Frith's photographs can be seen framed and as giant wall murals in thousands of pubs, restaurants, hotels, banks, retail stores and other public buildings throughout the country. In every case they enhance the unique local atmosphere of the places they depict and provide reminders of gentler days in an increasingly busy and frenetic world.

Product Promotions

Frith products are used by many major companies to promote the sales of their own products or to reinforce their own history and heritage. Frith promotions have been used by Hovis bread, Courage beers, Scots Porage Oats, Colman's mustard, Cadbury's foods, Mellow Birds coffee, Dunhill pipe tobacco, Guinness, and Bulmer's Cider.

Genealogy and Family History

As the interest in family history and roots grows world-wide, more and more people are turning to Frith's photographs of Great Britain for images of the towns, villages and streets where their ancestors lived; and, of course, photographs of the churches and chapels where their ancestors were christened, married and buried are an essential part of every genealogy tree and family album.

Frith Products

All Frith photographs are available Framed or just as Mounted Prints and Posters (size 23 x 16 inches). These may be ordered from the address below. From time to time other products - Address Books, Calendars, Table Mats, etc - are available.

The Internet

Already ninety thousand Frith photographs can be viewed and purchased on the internet through the Frith websites and a myriad of partner sites.

For more detailed information on Frith companies and products, look at these sites:

www.francisfrith.co.uk
www.francisfrith.com
(for North American visitors)

See the complete list of Frith Books at:

www.francisfrith.co.uk

This web site is regularly updated with the latest list of publications from The Francis Frith Collection. If you wish to buy books relating to another part of the country that your local bookshop does not stock, you may purchase on-line.

For further information, trade, or author enquiries please contact us at the address below:
The Francis Frith Collection, Frith's Barn, Teffont, Salisbury, Wiltshire, England SP3 5QP.
Tel: +44 (0)1722 716 376 Fax: +44 (0)1722 716 881 Email: sales@francisfrith.co.uk

See Frith books on the internet at www.francisfrith.co.uk

FREE PRINT OF YOUR CHOICE

Mounted Print
Overall size 14 x 11 inches (355 x 280mm)

Choose any Frith photograph in this book.
Simply complete the Voucher opposite and
return it with your remittance for £2.25 (to cover
postage and handling) and we will print the
photograph of your choice in SEPIA (size 11 x
8 inches) and supply it in a cream mount with a
burgundy rule line (overall size 14 x 11 inches).
**Please note: photographs with a reference
number starting with a "Z" are not Frith
photographs and cannot be supplied under
this offer.**
Offer valid for delivery to one UK address only.

PLUS: **Order additional Mounted Prints
at HALF PRICE - £7.49 each** (normally £14.99)
If you would like to order more Frith prints from
this book, possibly as gifts for friends and family,
you can buy them at half price (with no
additional postage and handling costs).

PLUS: **Have your Mounted Prints framed**
For an extra £14.95 per print you can have your
mounted print(s) framed in an elegant pol-
ished wood and gilt moulding, overall size 16 x
13 inches (no additional postage and handling
required).

IMPORTANT!

**These special prices are only available if you use
this form to order . You must use the ORIGINAL
VOUCHER on this page (no copies permitted). We
can only despatch to one UK address. This offer
cannot be combined with any other offer.**

Send completed Voucher form to:
**The Francis Frith Collection, Frith's Barn,
Teffont, Salisbury, Wiltshire SP3 5QP**